BUSINESS IN A BOX

YOUR GUIDE TO START, GROW, AND SCALE YOUR VIRTUAL FIRM

For Bookkeepers & Tax Professionals

by Lily Tran,
EA, CTC, NTPI Fellow

Disclaimer

Business in a Box: Your Guide to Start, Grow, and Scale Your Virtual Firm is an introductory guide to help you set up a U.S.-based small business correctly, being tax compliant and having a strong financial foundation.

This book does not provide binding tax, legal, or financial advice. The materials provided have been prepared for informational purposes only, and are not intended to provide tax, legal, or financial instructions as a substitute for a personal consultation. The material herein may not reflect the most current legislative or regulatory requirements, or the requirements of specific industries, or of specific states. These materials are not to be used for purposes of avoiding tax payments or tax penalties that may be imposed on a taxpayer. Readers should consult their own certified and professional tax, legal, and financial advisors before applying the laws or their interpretation of the laws to their specific situations.

This book is part of a series of tax guidance and support books for small business owners and fellow financial and tax professionals. Most of the topics covered in this book are a continuation of the topics that I introduced and detailed in the other books of this series, titled,

The Most Common Tax Mistakes Made by Small Businesses
by Lily Tran, EA, CTC, NTPI Fellow

Tax MythBusters: Don't Fall Prey to the Tax Misconceptions
Lily Tran, EA, CTC, NTPI Fellow

* Coming soon!

I highly recommend getting a copy of **The Most Common Tax Mistakes Made by Small Businesses** to serve as a companion guide to this book as I refer to various chapters to further explain topics and provide detailed examples, diagrams, charts, and pricing.

All my books are available on my website at www.taxusign.com or online.

INTRODUCTION

Like millions of people, I had dreams of leaving my job and running my own successful business while raising my son, but in the beginning, I didn't have enough time for either. I was rushing off in the mornings to set up my workstation in local credit union conference rooms or coffee shops, working with my clients one on one. If clients were late or canceled, I had no choice but to sit and wait until my next client showed up an hour later. Then, at the end of the day, I rushed home to make dinner and spend a few minutes with my family before bedtime, only to wake up the next day to start again. This cycle was exhausting, depleting, and very unfulfilling.

When I had my daughter, I wanted to be with her all the time and leaving her to meet with clients was really hard. I wanted to find a new way to be present for my family while serving my clients and my business.

After some investigation, I realized that working from home was something I could do with the right equipment, software solutions, and modifications to my business operations. Even as an enrolled agent, a certified tax coach, and NTPI fellow who specializes in tax planning and tax representation, I could set up a home office and run my business completely online. I will share my journey of establishing a virtual firm pre-COVID, scaling it nationwide with a team, and how I manage to enjoy vacations, like our 2022 family trip to Hawaii during the height of tax season. You can live this dream come true too. I will teach you how to effectively work remotely from anywhere, expand your services, connect with professionals all over the world, and build a business where you have both financial and time freedom.

This book outlines everything you need to know to stop the cycle of running your business in coffee shops and borrowed spaces to serving clients in the comfort of your virtual office at home or around the world. We will answer questions like:

- How do I know if this is right for me?
- What do I need to know to get started?
- What hardware and software do I need to run my business?
- How do I keep my clients' information safe and secure?
- How do I find new clients if I am working from home?
- How do I onboard them into my business?
- How do I communicate with them?
- How do I bring on employees when it is time?

The goal of this book is to help you identify your unique needs, and then build a viable and vibrant business that allows you to feel professionally fulfilled, and give you time to spend with the people you love doing things that bring you great joy. I'm excited to show you how to make that happen!

PART I

SETTING UP YOUR BUSINESS PROPERLY

Chapter 1: Business Plans

Sometimes when we think of creating a small business venture, it is easy to let our excitement build, and we get caught up in the possibilities of its greatness. While running a business is a blend of passion and dedication, it also needs a healthy amount of practicality.

What is the goal of the business?
What skills are needed to reach the goal?
When is it most likely you can reach the goal?
What resources are needed to attain the goal?
Who can assist or contribute to you reaching the goal?
How much time, energy, or money is needed to meet the goal?
What might stand in your way of reaching or surpassing your goal?
Where else can you secure funding or investments to pursue the goal?

It is hard to keep all of these questions and answers organized when they are in your head, but luckily there is a way to map it all out: a business plan.

Benjamin Franklin said, 'If you fail to plan, you are planning to fail.' While there are some businesses that start without a business plan, part of the reason nearly 80% of small business startups fail is that they don't have a comprehensive business plan that gets them thinking about all the parts of their business before they open up to customers.

A business plan is a formal written document that contains the answers to the above questions, as well as other key components like competitive analyses, financial projections, and market evaluations. While they are flexible in their design, they often ask strategic questions that ensure the business owner understands the market, the regulations, the competition, and how their business solves problems in their space.

If you search online for business plan templates, you will find options for every business in every industry. On the next page, you can see one possibility to get you started, though it is recommended to complete a more comprehensive business plan to fully understand all parts of your business venture.

BUSINESS PLAN

Purpose of a Business Plan

The purpose of a business plan is to document your company's objectives (the reason the world needs your products or services) and how your company plans to achieve its goals of growth and success.

A business plan is a document that can be used in many stages of your business. In the beginning, it can help you start laying out the foundation of your business and detail the expected financial, sales, and operation structures which allows you to see your business venture from a 360° view. It also is a common requirement for banks and investors during finance negotiations.

After your business begins, a business plan can help you determine if there are changes to be made in services or product offerings, or possible expansion through market growth or franchising.

By planning, you will most likely to succeed than fail. The business plan allows you to consider all possible factors that may affect your business and help you make better decisions.

WHAT IS THE EXECUTIVE SUMMARY?

- **Mission Statement**

  The mission statement is the company's purpose.

- **Business Description and Goals**

  This is where you list your short and long term goals that you want to achieve and accomplish.

- **Owner Qualifications and Experience**

  This is where you list your qualifications and experience.

BUSINESS PLAN TEMPLATE

Executive Summary

- Mission Statement: _____
  _____
  _____

- Business Description & Goals: _____
  _____
  _____

- Owner Qualifications & Experience: _____
  _____
  _____

Industry Environment

Overview of the Industry

a. _____
b. _____
c. _____
d. _____
e. _____

Potential Clients

a. _____
b. _____
c. _____
d. _____
e. _____

Direct Competitors

a. _____
b. _____
c. _____
d. _____
e. _____

Marketing

Overview of Products / Services

a. _____
b. _____
c. _____
d. _____
e. _____

Company Strategy

a. _____
b. _____
c. _____
d. _____
e. _____

Operations

Organizational Structure & Operating Plan

_____
_____
_____
_____
_____
_____
_____
_____
_____
_____
_____

Chapter 2: Business Entity

Choosing the incorrect entity structure due to a lack of understanding is very common. It is important to work with a qualified tax professional to choose the best entity structure for your business and to ensure the correct tax forms are completed and filed. The various business structure types include:

- Sole Proprietor
- Limited Liability Corporation (LLC)
- General Partnerships
- Limited Partnerships
- Limited Liability Partnerships
- Corporations
- S Corporations

In this book, we will focus on business owners in the first two entities (sole proprietorships and LLCs) because this is where most small business owners start their entrepreneurial journey. Since these emerging entrepreneurs often start their businesses without a team or advisors, they have a higher risk of making costly tax mistakes.

Every U.S. state has a government agency responsible for authorizing the formation and registration of business entities. These state agencies have different requirements, forms, and fees, so it is essential to know what business structure will be best for your situation so you can set up your business correctly from the start. Generally, the government filing document will require the name and address of the business, the name of the business owner, and other details depending on the business entity.

Sole proprietorships are the most common form of legal structure for small businesses. This business entity is owned and run by one individual with no legal distinction between the owner and the business. The owner is entitled to all profits and is fully responsible for all business debts or liabilities.

Recently, more and more people on social media are claiming that starting an S-Corporation is the best way to avoid paying taxes. This is not true. S-Corps have specific requirements that must be followed, and there is a chart for this business entity at the end of this chapter.

SOLE PROPRIETORSHIP

Unincorporated business owned by one individual. The sole proprietorship is the most common business entity. It is not a legal entity separate and apart from its owner.

Advantages:

- Easy and relatively inexpensive to form
- Few government regulations
- Lower income taxes than other forms of business

Limitations:

- Unlimited personal liability
- Short business life
- More challenging to attract large capital

LIMITED LIABILITY COMPANY (LLC)

An LLC is a state-recognized entity that may allow you to operate your business as a sole proprietor, however, there are other entities that your business might be better suited for, so consulting a tax professional would help you make the right choice in your setup. The IRS will view the single-member LLC business as a sole proprietorship.

One of the benefits of having an LLC includes personal protection. Personal protection is one of the main reasons small business owners opt for this business structure, as LLCs protect you from personal liability in most instances, and, unlike a sole proprietorship, your personal assets, like your house, car, and savings, won't be at risk if your LLC faces a lawsuit or bankruptcy.

A business structure in the United States whereby the owners are not personally liable for the company's debts or liabilities. LLCs are hybrid entities that combine the characteristics of a corporation with those of a partnership or sole proprietorship.

Advantages:

- Complete pass-through tax advantages and operational flexibility of a partnership.
- Corporation-style limited liability under state law.
- No restrictions on the number or types of members.
- Management participation by all members where members are the owners or shareholders of the LLC.

Limitations:

- Some states do not allow professional groups to operate through an LLC
- Transferability restrictions – consent of membership is required for each and every transfer of membership interests
- Cannot make a public stock offering

SINGLE-MEMBER LIMITED LIABILITY COMPANIES

Generally treated as a disregarded entity unless it elects to be taxed as a corporation.

Advantages:

- It is no longer attached to and identified with the owner for tax or liability purposes.
- The SMLLC is formed within a state and part of the approval process is a registration of the business name, so no other business in the state may use that name.

Limitations:

- SMLLCs face reduced asset protection. Many states do not honor asset protection for LLCs with a single owner.

S-CORPORATIONS

The S corporation is a special type of corporation created as a business form in 1958.

Advantages:

- Not taxed: the income is taxed to shareholders when earned by the S corporation.
- Limited liability

Limitations:

- Several ownership restrictions placed on this entity
- More administrative duties required
- Single class of stock with per share, per day income allocation

PARTNERSHIP

A legal arrangement between two or more people.

Advantages:

- Easy and inexpensive to form
- Avoid corporate income tax

Limitations:

- Unlimited personal liability to all partners
- Difficult to raise large capital

CORPORATION

It separates owners and managers. Regular corporations are referred to as C corps.

Advantages:

- Limited liability for stockholders
- Unlimited lives
- Easy to transfer shares
- Therefore, easy to attract a large amount of capital

Limitations:

- Double taxation: corporation income tax and dividend tax

BUSINESS ENTITY: Various Business Structure Types

	Summary	Tax Forms & Applicable Publications
Sole Proprietorship	• Simple business entity. • No need to separate business entity from personal entity for tax purposes.	Schedule C
Limited Liability Company (LLC)	• Typically register in your home state but there are reasons to register your LLC in another state instead. • The rules for LLC compliance vary from state to state. • Provides personal protection from litigation • More expensive to set up than Sole Proprietorships.	
General Partnerships	• Option when two or more people in business together • Set-up is often straightforward and inexpensive. • Profits are generally subject to self-employment taxes. • All partners are personally liable for everything pertaining to the business and its operations.	
Limited Partnerships (LPs)	• At least one partner must assume liability for the whole company. • LPs are less complicated to set up than corporations, LLCs, or LLPs • Offers total liability protection for all limited partners. • More expensive to set up than General Partnerships.	Form 1065 / IRS Pub. 541
Limited Liability Partnerships (LLPs)	• LLPs do not pay federal taxes. • This entity provides liability protection. • No general partner is needed to assume all risk. • Expensive to set up properly. • LLP rules are different in each state. • Profits are subject to self-employment taxes and are taxed whether all income is distributed or not.	

BUSINESS ENTITY
The Various Business Structure Types

	Summary	Tax Forms & Applicable Publications
C-Corporations	• Limited liability for directors, shareholders, and other company officers. • C corps can raise capital by issuing and selling shares of stock. • C Corporations must register with the SEC upon reaching certain thresholds. • This entity is subject to greater regulation than other business structures, typically incurring higher legal fees due to its complexity. • Shareholders cannot deduct their losses, and business profits are double-taxed as dividends are issued.	Form 1120 / IRS Pub. 542
S-Corporations	• Tax benefits: no or lesser corporate and self-employment tax for owner, no double taxation for shareholders • Protections of incorporation: limited liability, transfer of interests • Prestige, credibility • Expensive Incorporation Costs • Complex compliance rules • Potentially growth-inhibiting qualifications to maintain status	Form 1120S / IRS Pub. 542

Notes

S-Corporation Compliance Checklist

- ☐ Establish and maintain reasonable shareholder compensation
- ☐ Make careful, diligent decisions in distributing cash and property to
- ☐ shareholders
- ☐ Establish and maintain an accountable reimbursement plan for all employees
- ☐ Establish and maintain basis schedules for all shareholders
- ☐ Establish and maintain proper loan agreements between S Corp and
- ☐ shareholders
- ☐ Establish and maintain bookkeeping on at least a monthly basis
- ☐ Establish and maintain payroll compliance at a minimum frequency of monthly

    File annual tax returns timely and accurately

- ☐ Establish and maintain retirement and benefit programs with required

    compliance for S Corporation shareholders

    Bonus: Establish and maintain a corporate binder with annual board meetings

    and corporate minutes

This S-Corp checklist is an excerpt from the chapter "Jumping into S Corp Too Fast" by Jamie E. O'Kane, CPA, CTC, in <u>The Most Common Tax Mistakes Made by Small Businesses</u> by Lily Tran, EA, CTC, NTPI Fellow.

Notes

Chapter 3: Business Licenses

Now that you have decided on your business entity, you need a business license. This is a very commonly overlooked area of business setup, partly because there are so many layers to it depending on your business, your city, county, and state. In fact, there are more than 100,000 different jurisdictions across the country, and each has its own required licenses and permits. Every business, industry, state, and city has different regulations in place. Even if you start searching online for what you need, you might find yourself confused or even missing out on key licenses that your business needs.

What is a business license?

Business licenses are formal permits issued by a local government agency to authorize individuals or small business owners to conduct business within the government's geographic district. A single business in a single location might require multiple licenses issued by multiple government departments and agencies.

Oftentimes, entrepreneurs think only certain businesses need licenses, like those serving food or alcohol. In fact, it is a very common mistake that small businesses do not apply for all the appropriate licenses, but every business requires a business license, or several, because of the requirements to meet city, state, and federal laws.

You will find the business license requirements within your state Department of Revenue and local cities. Check every city that you operate your business in, whether a city business license is required. For example, if you have two stores in two locations in your state, each one could require a separate city license from the city it is located.

Common Licenses

Here are the most common licenses entrepreneurs maintain:

Federal – Most businesses won't need a federal license. However, if you are selling products or services regulated by the federal government, you may need a license from the appropriate federal agency before you start. Some examples of these businesses include those in industries like agriculture, alcohol or tobacco, aviation, fisheries, firearms and explosives, broadcasting, mining, transportation, and imports from foreign countries.

State – States regulate a broader range of commercial activities than the federal government, so most entrepreneurs will need to have a business license issued by their state to conduct business in the state. Some examples of industries requiring state licensing include retail, restaurants, trades like plumbing and construction, and businesses in the financial industry and beauty industry.

City – Almost every city requires a business to be licensed by the city annually if you have a business based in the city and/or are conducting business within city limits. Some neighboring cities require you to have an active business license if you visit occasionally and conduct business, in addition to the city where your business is based.

Professional License – There are some businesses that require the person conducting the service to be licensed in their profession. These occupational licenses may include realtors; pet caretakers; food service providers; personal care service providers like hairdressers, barbers, and estheticians; and daycare/childcare and education providers.

Sales Tax License – This license may also be called a sales tax permit in some states. It is an agreement with the state tax agency that the business owner will collect and remit sales tax on items sold by the business. With this license, the entrepreneur is required to collect local and state tax in the state that issues the license, and then remit the collected tax money to the proper tax authority. This affects in-person and online sales. Examples of this for your business might include digital tax checklists for your clients, books or workbooks you create, or branded merchandise like calculators or pens.

There are many other licenses that must be secured depending on the type of business you own, such as liquor license, sales tax license, and a variety of professional licenses. Research what is required in your city, state, and in your profession to stay compliant in this area.

Chapter 4: Employer Identification Number

After you secure your business licenses, you will need to apply for an Employer Identification Number (EIN) through the IRS website.

What is an employer identification number?

An EIN is a nine-digit number assigned by the IRS also known as a Federal Tax Identification Number, and is used to identify a business entity for tax purposes. This EIN is used in place of your Social Security Number (SSN). You will receive a letter from the IRS containing your EIN. This number will stay with your business until you cancel your EIN number to close your business. If you are a sole proprietorship business, you are not required to apply for an EIN.

Applying for an IRS Employer Identification Number is free. You can apply online, by fax, or by mail. Please visit the IRS website to get more information and apply:

https://www.irs.gov/businesses/small-businesses-self-employed/apply-for-an-employer- identification-number-ein-online

EMPLOYER IDENTIFICATION NUMBER (EIN)
To-Do List and Questionnaire

☐ 1. Legal name, entity (or individual) for the EIN request: _____

☐ 2. Trade name of the business (if different from #1): _____

☐ 3. Address of business location: _____

☐ 4. Mailing address: _____

☐ 5. Responsible party: _____

☐ 6. Type of entity: _____

Notes

Chapter 5: Business Insurance

Many small business owners, especially those who work from home, might believe that they don't need business insurance because they don't have a physical location where someone could fall and hurt themselves, but they would be incorrect. Even if you work remotely or don't have a physical office space, you still need liability insurance to protect you and your business from costs associated with claims or lawsuits. Liability insurance provides coverage for more than slip-and-falls and property damage; if a client is unhappy with the outcome of your delivered service or a product you sold causes an unwanted result, you may find yourself on the wrong side of a lawsuit.

For example, what happens if your client claims you didn't deliver the financial outcome you promised in their annual tax filing and they sue you? Or what about if you made an honest mistake in a calculation that led to financial loss for them? Insurance protects you against lawsuits associated with risks that our specific work entails.

Depending on your needs, a business liability insurance policy can include the following coverages:

- <u>Professional liability insurance</u> is a type of liability insurance that provides coverage for claims alleging negligence or failure to deliver a service as promised, resulting in financial loss.
- <u>Errors and omissions insurance</u> is a type of professional liability insurance that protects you from claims alleging a financial loss due to an error or omission on your part.
- <u>Cyber liability insurance</u> covers the costs associated with recovering from a cybercrime involving your technology systems and customer data.

Business insurance can be deducted from your taxes if it is considered both ordinary and necessary to your company's operation. The vast majority of modern businesses are required to carry some form of business insurance due to state laws, industry regulations, or requirements in contracts.

For a more comprehensive guide to business insurance, please refer to chapter two of *The Common Tax Mistakes Made by Small Businesses* , by Lily Tran.

BUSINESS INSURANCE
Business Insurance Policy Types

	Summary
General Liability	Coverage every business needs
Commercial Auto	Covers all vehicles of a small business
Key Man Life Insurance	Life insurance written on the owners to help protect the company from their untimely death and the financial impact their passing may have.
Commercial Package Policy (CPP)	A package of two or more coverages like general liability, equipment breakdown, inland marine, commercial auto liability, and commercial property.
Business Owners Policy (BOP)	Business property combined with business liability with additional endorsements pertinent to your business need.
Professional Liability	Covers negligence, misrepresentation, and inaccurate advice when conducting business
Inland Marine	Helps cover products, materials, and equipment while it is transported to and from a job site or related to a business event.
Workers Compensation	Benefits your employees if they get injured or become ill due to working on the job.

Notes

BUSINESS INSURANCE
What I Need and What Is Offered By Insurance Companies

	My Needs	Insurer 1	Insurer 2
Liability			
• Deductible			
• Annual Premium			
• Policy Limits			
Business Interruption			
• Deductible			
• Annual Premium			

Other _____			

www.taxusign.com

Chapter 6: Bank Accounts

Next, take your business license and EIN letter to open a business bank account. Check with your bank to see if any other documents are required before you open your business bank account. I recommend opening at least two bank accounts, one for checking and one for savings. You want to set money aside in your savings account for taxes. As a business owner, the one rule you must follow is to never commingle funds.

What are Commingling Funds?

Commingling funds is when a business owner mixes business and personal funds together. This is one of the biggest issues small business owners have because they don't realize how important it is to keep business money separate from personal money. On the surface, they might think that it shouldn't matter because all the money is going to the same person at the end of the day—but the IRS does not see it this way.

What does it look like to commingle funds? It might be depositing a business check into a personal account or paying for a personal expense with a business credit card. Either way, it is important to keep your business and personal finances separate to avoid the IRS from questioning the integrity of the business entity or the transactions.

Account Reconciliation

By December 31 of each year, it's vital to reconcile your income, expenses, and fees. As a small business owner, you are responsible to manage the financial side of your business in order to be compliant with tax regulations. How do you do that? By accurately and consistently tracking all activities in your business as they happen when the details are accurate.

This is vital for you as a business owner to do and to model for your clients who must understand the rules about tracking, documenting, organizing and managing their finances. Setting your clients up for business success starts with setting a good example for money management and avoiding commingling funds and finances.

BUSINESS ACCOUNTS
Documents to Open an Account

☐ 1. Business Name and Tradenames: _____

☐ 2. Employer Identification Number: _____

☐ 3. Address of business location: _____

☐ 4. Mailing address: _____

☐ 5. Business License: _____

☐ 6. Operating Agreement _____

☐ 7. Driver's License or Passport _____

Notes

PART II

SETTING UP YOUR VIRTUAL OFFICE

Chapter 7: The Right Equipment

One term that has been surging in online search results over the last few years is *'laptop lifestyle,'* referring to the 'location-freedom' that some entrepreneurs and small business owners can enjoy when they provide services that can be completed from anywhere. Tax and accounting professionals can be part of this group, provided they have one of the most important requirements: having the right equipment.

In running your business, there are several mandatory pieces of equipment you will need to communicate with your clients, access their secured financial files, perform required research to work on their requests, complete their projects, and maintain accurate administrative records. As well, there are items that will support the non-client facing work required in your business.

Before we identify the list of equipment, however, we need to consider where you will be working most often. If you are working from a home office, you can have stationary items like a desktop computer, printers and scanners, and multiple monitors. What if you are working in various places? Your equipment will need to be more portable, yet powerful and functional to do your work. One consideration for people living the *laptop lifestyle* is that many cities around the world offer co-working spaces that rent desks, cubicles, or offices on a monthly or annual basis, giving you a professional workspace outside of your home and offering a quiet, focused work area, access to printers and scanners, an address separate from your home address, and community with other business owners.

Here is a starting list of equipment that you should consider necessities for running your venture with ease and professionalism:

- Powerful laptop or computer (tablets don't always have enough processing power or internal storage capacity)
- High-quality monitor
- High-speed internet connection
- Headphones or ear buds for private conversations
- Microphone for meetings (if this is not a feature of your headphones)
- Calculator that performs functions you need most often
- Data storage equipment, like an external hard drive
- Printer if forms require pen signatures and not digital signatures
- Scanner (if you aren't using your cell phone or a mobile app)

Now that you have learned the essential equipment, let's discuss the strategy for converting your in-person clients into virtual clients.

When I made the decision to transition to a virtual firm, I sent an initial email to inform my clients about the portal I'm setting up for them. This direct communication with each client ensured they recognize the change as a legitimate email rather than spam.

As I heard back from every client and answered any questions they had, I guided them through the process of setting up their account and gave them a tutorial about using the portal. I showed them how to access their information, where to upload their data, where to download forms, and other related tasks. Investing in each client was possible because I rolled out my transition in a methodical and intentional way. It was important to me to partner with each client through this process instead of expecting them to figure it out on their own. Especially in the industry of tax, finance, and accounting, maintaining trust is paramount.

Rolling out the change to my clients was a big milestone in this process to move to a virtual business, but it wasn't the first, or the second big project. In fact, it was near the end! There are many components that were required to make this transition to virtual office a success, however you don't have to figure it out on your own. In the following pages, we will explore the platforms and tools that efficiently manage my practice, my clients, daily and weekly tasks, plus those that maintain accurate documentation, and help with team building and collaboration.

Chapter 8: Customer Relationship Management Systems

<u>Customer relationship management (CRM)</u> is an online database that provides small business owners a simple and straightforward way to stay connected to clients, streamline their communication processes, and stay top of mind with their audience.

Client emails can be entered into your CRM database so you can send out timely reminders, like deadlines or appointments. Many small business owners also create a general newsletter for anyone who signs up, which contain updates about the financial or tax industry, and your opinions on what is relevant to your audience, such as changes to tax codes or new regulations.

One major benefit of most CRM systems is customization. You can set up your CRM system so that each contact is assigned to a category, like Current Clients, Prospective Clients, Past Clients, General Interest, or other groups. When you create an email, announcement, reminder, or newsletter, you then select who receives it based on how they are connected to your business. This way, you are giving the right people the right information to build and deepen your relationship with them.

Another benefit of a robust CRM system is efficiency. Imagine two years ago, you created a financial planning toolkit. It's now today, and you have updated it to be more comprehensive, including new worksheets and planning guides. How do you find the people who are most likely to purchase the new version? Well, you would start with the people who bought the original version since they would be most likely to upgrade their toolkit. Since you love efficiency, you can go into your CRM system where these original clients were assigned to the category called *ToolKit Clients,* and you can write one email and send it to all of them announcing the updated version and provide a link to purchase. They get an incredible product, and you reach the right people with the right solution. Win-win!

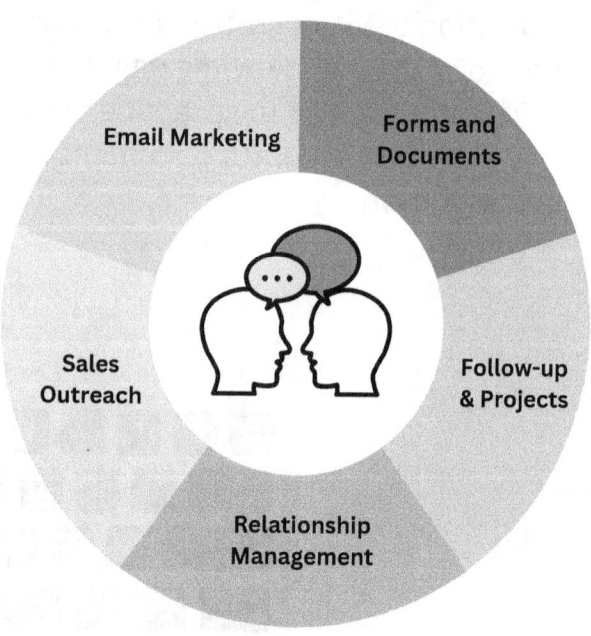

Customer Relationship Management

In the tax and finance space, there are many options for CRM systems that can be customized to meet your unique needs. Here are two great options.

TaxDome is designed for those in the tax and accounting industry, and helps you manage your tax practice workflow, billing, time tracking, and provides a secure client portal. One other benefit is being able to access ready-made templates (bookkeeping, tax returns, payroll, resolution and more) or create your own customizable, repeatable business processes that enable you to take your firm to the next level. If you want to explore more, go to: https://taxdome.com/?fp_ref=taxusign

GQueues is the leading task manager built specifically for Google Workspace. Google Docs is for writing communications and documents, Gmail is for email, and GQueues is for managing your team's work. This planning, organizing, and prioritization tool makes sure nothing falls through the cracks. If you want to see if this tool will help you in your business, go to https://gqz.page.link/VmjeMESC9RjFqNZu9

For many small business owners, Microsoft Excel and other free tools are the first software systems used to start their business operations. Some stay with those systems for years, and others decide they want a more robust, customizable, and scalable solution. If you would like to explore other CRM systems for planning, tracking, billing, or managing client and business operations, you can consider these companies:

TaxDome	GQueues
Ignition	pipedrive
HubSpot	monday.com
dubsado	Zoho
Liscio	

Chapter 9: Administrative Software Options

Many small business owners are surprised by how much administration is required in a day. Here is a glossary of some admin software solutions, with more detailed explanations and market information on the following pages.

VPN	Have you found yourself at Starbucks or in a hotel conference using public Wi-Fi? If you're not using a Virtual Private Network, or VPN, in such situations, you could unknowingly transmit confidential client information over the public network. During tax season when I spent a week in Kauai, I brought my laptop along. Whenever I needed to use public Wi-Fi, I made sure to activate my VPN for added security. Essentially, a VPN connection establishes a secure connection between your computer and an encrypted network to protect your data and disguise your IP address so no one can identify your location or your online activities on public Wi-Fi. Following this chart, I provide more details about VPN specifically.
Digital Signatures	Privacy and security are non-negotiable when you have a virtual office. Digital signature software enables your clients to safely sign contracts and legal documents. Gone are the days when you need to drive to your client's location for a signature. Nowadays, there are companies that capture digital signatures for legal and financial contracts without anyone meeting in person.
Portals	Portals offer secure, web- or cloud-based document management & storage solutions meeting needs in security, compliance, and workflow. If you opt to create a portal for your clients, each client will only see and access their own account, while you and your team can see all your clients accounts and data.
Remote Access	Remote access tools enable connections between two or more computer or network nodes and are typically installed on local computers.

Chapter 9: Administrative Software Options

Backup Drives	One issue you do not want to have is data loss. Backup drives create file management redundancy in case of computer malfunction or other digital problems, as well as provide timelines for additions in case of audit. Saving backup, duplicate copies of all client contracts, files, and documents ensures uninterrupted access.
Virtual Communication	Various options exist for communicating with clients and others via text, voice, or video.
Scheduling Appointments	Remove the need for email or phone tag to find a time both you and your client are available. Online calendars and booking tools help your clients peruse your calendar openings and book time with you, and allow you to track meetings and document time spent with clients for billing or time management purposes.
Fax	Even though email has replaced many communication interactions, fax is still required by some government, financial, medical, and legal organizations.
Digital Scanner	There are many instances where paper documents need to be scanned to be sent or stored digitally.

SETTING UP YOUR VIRTUAL OFFICE
VIRTUAL PRIVATE NETWORK (VPN)

COMPARISON BENEFITS FOR VPN

	NORDVPN	PRIVATE INTERNET ACCESS
OVERVIEW	**NordVPN** packs top-notch protection and other privacy features into a slick client, powered by the latest VPN technology. It's a privacy juggernaut, at a premium price.	**PIA** offers a robust VPN service with advanced network settings, an excellent app interface, and strong speeds. Its features go beyond VPN protection but requires confirmation.
PROS	• Uses WireGuard VPN technology • Multi-hop, split tunneling • Numerous server locations • Strong customer privacy stance • Easy to use	• Well designed app • 10 simultaneous connections • Numerous server locations • Advanced network settings • Excellent speed test scores
CONS	• Expensive • Occasionally cramped interface	• Unusual login system • No free version
	PROTON VPN	**MCAFEE SAFE CONNECT**
OVERVIEW	**Proton VPN** offers the best free subscription tiers, and its paid tiers provide access to numerous privacy tools at a reasonable price.	**MSC** is a US-based VPN service with Windows, iOS, and Android apps. With dynamic IP addresses that change every time you connect, this VPN makes you nearly impossible to trace online.
PROS	• Best free subscription • Numerous advanced privacy tools • Strong customer privacy stance • Slick, accessible client • Excellent Speedtest scores	• Very fast speeds • Appealing and intuitive apps • Dedicated apps for PC, Android, and iOS
CONS	• Awkward Chrome OS integration • Complicated pricing structure	• Less features than competitors • Only 18 virtual servers

SETTING UP YOUR VIRTUAL OFFICE
DIGITAL SIGNATURES - TAXDOME

Privacy and security are non-negotiable when you are setting up and running a virtual office. How do you have clients sign contracts, legal documents, and other forms when you are not in the same room? By using a digital signature that is captured and applied by a company that offers this popular feature. Here are some of the most popular options for digital signature management. Use the link here to receive 2 free subscription months when you sign up:
https://taxdome.com/?fp_ref=taxusign

When collecting electronic signatures for tax services, it's crucial to prioritize Knowledge-Based Authentication (KBA) to verify the client's identity. Here are both options with and without KBA compliant software such as these below:

Adobe Sign
Dropbox Sign (formerly HelloSign)
DocuSign
SignNow
Preview
eSignatures.io
SignWell
signNow

SETTING UP YOUR VIRTUAL OFFICE
PORTAL - TAXDOME

A portal will help you exchange documents with clients securely. I use TaxDome as an all-in-one solution that covers multiple aspects of my virtual office.

Easy to use custom-branded accounting client portal software
- Easy to use
- Secure communication
- Share and sign documents electronically
- Invoicing
- Fully Custom Branded
- Automate new client onboarding
- Automated workflow & predictable outcome
- Easy & secure access
- White-glove Support & Training Sessions Included

Other Options:

Drake Portal
SmartVault
ShareFile
Onvio
Canopy
Verifyle

SETTING UP YOUR VIRTUAL OFFICE
REMOTE ACCESS - VERITO

How did I manage to travel and work remotely during tax season? I purchased a remote access which enabled me to take my laptop to Kauai and remotely connect to a server or computer to complete my work. Close your eyes, take a deep breath, and envision yourself feeling the sand beneath your feet, the warm sun shining down as you cherish quality time with your family during tax season. Doesn't that feel good?

Remote access tools enable connections between two or more computer or network nodes and are typically installed on local computers.

- Perform security updates
- Fix technical issues
- Update system settings for a remotely located computer/laptop

https://verito.com/

"Verito Technologies' cloud-based software is simply outstanding. From the moment we implemented it into our workflow, we witnessed a remarkable transformation in our operations. The intuitive interface makes it easy for our team to adapt and utilize its powerful features effectively. Verito's excellent customer support has been a great asset, promptly addressing any concerns or issues. We genuinely appreciate the value Verito Technologies brings to our business, and we wholeheartedly recommend it to anyone looking to optimize their operations and stay ahead in today's dynamic market." - Lily Tran, EA, CTC

RemotePC
Microsoft Remote Desktop
SplashTop
TeamViewer
Zoho Assist

verito

I've used various remote access tools, and from my experience, I've found Verito to be the best option. It not only enables me to access data from anywhere but also allows my team to collaborate and work simultaneously on a local computer. This flexibility and efficiency have been instrumental in running my virtual office effectively.

Have you ever encountered that heart-pounding moment when your computer crashes? To avoid such situations, it's wise to back up documents and you can use an external hard drive or these services below:

Livedrive: Ideal if you and your employees need a straightforward option, without requiring high computer savviness.

- Intuitive interface design is paired with great features.
- Good support for all desktop and mobile devices
- Automatic backup
- Real-time syncing
- Two-factor authentication and 256-bit encryption
- Packed with sharing tools
- Easy to use and navigate

Carbonite: Carbonite is an easy-to-use online backup provider with great security, privacy and customer support.

- Unlimited cloud storage
- Remote sharing and access
- Cloud backup
- Courier recovery
- Hybrid backup
- Backup policies customization and mirror image
- Video and hard drive backup
- It lets Windows users revert to a previous OS version in case of deletion/loss of data

IDrive: The popular iDrive cloud service offers a huge list of features, putting it in the clear lead for best cloud storage for business.

- Real-time syncing
- Multiple device backups
- Support for older file versions and 30-day retention of deleted files
- Available for iOS and Android
- 24/7 support
- Retrieve Data

SETTING UP YOUR VIRTUAL OFFICE
VIRTUAL COMMUNICATION

To meet your clients virtually, here are the popular options. Zoom is my favorite choice.

Zoom	• **Quality video meetings** • **Screen sharing, polling** • **Customized backgrounds** • **Scheduled meetings** • **Limited 40mins/meeting in Free version - no time limit above versions** • **Recording feature**
Microsoft Teams	• **Video conferencing, virtual events, audio conferencing** • **Instant Messaging** • **Screen sharing** • **Custom backgrounds** • **Unlimited 1:1 meetings for meetings up to 30 hours long** • **File sharing, tasks, and polling**
Google Meets	• **Anyone with a Google account can create a video meeting** • **Invite up to 100 participants** • **Meet for up 60 minutes/ meeting** • **International dial-in numbers** • **Meeting recordings can be automatically saved to Google drive.**

You don't want to miss out on scheduling clients because you want to make sure they receive the highest customer service at all times, but you don't want to be tied to your phone to schedule people into your calendar. Luckily, there are many online programs that allow clients to peruse your open slots and select the day and time that work best for them. Plus, they don't have to be restricted to booking appointments with you during your office hours. In fact, if a client wants to check your calendar in the middle of the night, they can do that without you even knowing! Online calendars allow you to open time slots for client appointments, and block time slots for already scheduled meetings, appointments, or even personal time.

Most online calendar tools have basic options, and many times those are free. However, to add your logo or colors, payment options, appointment confirmation emails, or other premium features, you will need to either subscribe or pay extra per month.

Here are some of the top choices right now to consider:

Square Appointments
Calendly
Google Calendar
Acuity Scheduling
Zoho Bookings
Wix

Fax machines were in almost every office in the 1980s and 1990s but have gradually become obsolete by Internet-based technologies such as digital scanning and email. If you find yourself sending several faxes a week, I highly recommend using an electronic fax services, which prove invaluable when needing to fax to the IRS the Form 8821 and/or Form 2848 while on the phone with them. Now, they only accept physical, handwritten signatures on a physical document - sometimes called a *wet signature* - on these forms when faxing. This is where the portal and scanner come in handy.

If you rarely send faxes, a free faxing service will do, but if you send many faxes or want customization and branding of the fax cover page, unlimited storage, having local or toll-free numbers, and sending to multiple recipients, you can look into premium fax services.

Below are some of the industry leaders:

eFax
HelloFax
FaxZero

SCANNER APPLICATIONS

For document scanning, apps such as below are recommended. Using a scanner app is a fantastic solution for clients who might not have access to a physical scanner or can't afford one. It's a cost-effective and efficient way for them to digitize their documents and securely upload them to the portal. If you decide to purchase a scanner, take a look at the Fujitsu ix500 ScanSnap.

Scanning your documents will allow you to properly and conveniently store your paper documents and receipts. It will also help make our work more efficient.

Here are some of our favorite apps for scanning documents:
1. **Notes (iOS)**
2. **Adobe Scan (iOS & Android)**
3. **Microsoft Office Lens (iOS & Android)**
4. **CamScanner (iOS & Android)**

Notes

Chapter 10: Accounting Software Options

If you have been in this industry for some time, you might remember the oversized, heavy transaction journals that covered most desks. Those days are over. Accounting software has become a staple for professionals who require speed, efficiency, and accuracy for their clients.

Accounting software is installed on your computer and helps manage all financial functions, including recording and reporting transactions, for businesses. Finance and accounting teams use the software's accounting tools to manage expenses and cash flow, as well as functions like billing, payroll, general ledger, accounts receivable, and accounts payable.

On top of financial management, accounting software makes accounting calculations easier to perform, understand, and analyze so recommendations can be done in a more efficient manner.

Additionally, accounting software allows small finance and tax professionals to digitize financial paperwork, which allows for the near-instantaneous reporting and analysis of data in different areas of the business. Plus, when you have your client's financial history in digital form, it is much easier to view old data or previous year's information to find trends or patterns that can guide their business decisions. And, in the case of an internal or external (IRS) audit, you can retrieve all of the submissions, receipts, and documents for your client with a few clicks on your computer.

If your business needs are very specific, or your small business grows bigger and you need a higher level of support, you might choose to invest in a more customized accounting software solution. For everyone else, they often start with a software that is readily available and easy to set up and use. Below, we review some of the top choices on the market today.

BENEFITS OF ACCOUNTING SOFTWARE

The benefits of using accounting software are many, including:

- Accuracy of calculations based on the data entered into the program
- Automation of some basic functions like rendering charts and tables
- Availability of documents and records from anywhere, anytime
- Invoice creation
- Report generation

In the early days of computerized accounting software, the benefit was the speed and accuracy of the calculation side of the work. However, now accounting software is much more sophisticated. Many of the major software companies provide options like automatic invoicing and follow-up, bank account reconciliation, invoice templates customized to each customer, inventory control in real time, customized reports and graphs using data in limitless ways, and manage employee wages, payroll taxes, and other payments.

Each software company offers the main accounting features, but some offer more premium features depending on your needs and your industry.

Before exploring all of the available options, make a list of what accounting functions matter to your business, and what information you need to maintain, grow, scale, and manage your full business operation.

_____

_____

_____

ACCOUNTING SOFTWARE

Using Excel: When you first start your business, you may not be generating income and you are searching for an affordable way to track your income and expenses, one way to do that is using Excel.

Choosing a More Robust Accounting Software: Whether you are just starting out or have been operating for some time, now is the time to purchase and use accounting software for your business. What used to take a lot of time, energy, and money can now be done quickly and easily with the click of a few buttons. Accounting and bookkeeping software enables you to connect your bank and credit card accounts capturing all transactions into the software system and allowing you to then properly designate each transaction to the right business category.

Xero
QuickBooks Online
Freshbooks
Sage
Drake Accounting
Excel
Zoho

ACCOUNTING SOFTWARE OPTIONS
RECEIPT MANAGEMENT

The running joke is how impossible it is to serve our clients well when they drop off a shoebox of receipts a week before the tax deadline. As a small business owner, you know the importance of keeping good financial records and having an accurate receipt management system, but many of our clients don't prioritize good record tracking and receipt management practices.

Knowing about digital receipt management systems can help you guide your clients to the best solutions for their lifestyle and their business operations, and save them time and money in your administrative fees.

Sometimes, clients who are freelancers or independent contractors think receipt management doesn't pertain to them, but everyone who files taxes needs to maintain accurate records of transactions.

While some people do sort, file, and maintain paper receipts and records, there are software tools and applications that help small business owners stay organized, keep track of deductions, and reduce tax errors with a few clicks.

So, we prepare this section, this chart will help you narrow down your decision.

Notes

Imagine you are going on a trip to the Amazon. Although you had lots of time to pack, you left it until the last minute making you rush through packing to make your flight. When you finally arrive in the jungle, you open your suitcase to find you packed high heels instead of hiking boots and perfume instead of bug spray. You had good intentions, but lacked a good packing list and a system to keep you organized and on track.

This happens all the time with clients who don't have good systems for receipt and document management. Instead of having everything in one place, they lose receipts and miss out on write-offs, they misfile paper documents and lose time searching high and low for them, and they work long hours typing everything into Excel instead of spending precious time with their family or friends. There is a better way!

Keeping receipts and documents meticulously organized and categorized is one of the best ways to reduce tax season stress, and ensure you are maximizing deductions and reducing taxable income. Here are some options for going digital with receipt management and deduction classification.

QuickBooks App	**Hubdoc**
Digitally	**Google Drive**
Portal	**Expensify**
Receipt Bank	

Chapter 11: Tax Software Options

The U.S. Tax Code, also known as the Internal Revenue Code, is the official body of law guiding all federal tax laws, enacted in Title 26 of the United States Code by the U.S. Congress. The law codifies all federal tax laws with sections that include income taxes, estate and gift taxes, employment taxes, alcohol, tobacco, and certain other excise taxes. The Internal Revenue Service (IRS) is the body responsible for implementing the tax laws through their Treasury regulations and revenue rulings.

One source states the U.S. Tax Code, published by Thomson Reuters, is around 2600 pages, while another source states a downloadable PDF from the IRS website prints on 6871 pages. While there is disagreement of its length, there is no argument that the document is huge, and quite complex.

As accountants and tax professionals, it is crucial that we know and understand the U.S. Tax Code so we can help our clients be in compliance with current laws and regulations, know what tax deductions and credits are available to them, and to avoid penalties from the IRS.

Luckily, we don't have to memorize the tax code to serve our clients because some companies have created specific tax software to help us along the way.

Tax software is a type of computer software designed to help individuals or companies prepare for and file income, corporate and similar tax returns. It streamlines the process of filing taxes by walking the user through tax forms and issues and also automatically calculates the individual's or company's tax obligations.

These software options are designed with up-to-date rules and regulations for your specific tax year. They can provide you with the forms required for your income tax submission, and they can calculate what you owe or what type of return you'll be receiving.

While these software options have robust capabilities, they cannot and do not replace the experience or expertise of a professional financial or tax expert. Tax software is not perfect nor 100% capable of discerning all the nuances of our client's tax circumstances so they should be a tool to help expedite the tax completion process, but not the only source of information.

TAX SOFTWARES

Online tax software can help you file taxes by guiding you through the process and double-checking to ensure you've filled out all of the necessary tax forms for your filing status and situation. Most tax software options offer similar options, but many companies differentiate by offering unique add-ons. Here are some industry leaders:

Drake	• Shortcut keys and macros • Automatic data flow • Multi-state returns • Access online tax research • Update prior-year data • Import and Export • Tax planner • Print to PDF & Attach PDFs • Drake E-Sign
UltraTax	• Data sharing • Electronic filing • Document & Asset management • Advanced tax planning capabilities • Multi-State • Mobile devices
Lacerte	• User-friendly Interface • Comprehensive Form Library • Hassle-free E-Organizer • E-Signature • Error Diagnostics and Automated Calculations • Integration Capabilities • Trial Balance Utility • Tax Analysis and Planning Tools • Intuit Link

TAX SOFTWARES

TaxSlayer	<ul><li>Easy to use</li><li>TaxesToGo mobile app (NOT include in Classic package)</li><li>Free unlimited filing</li><li>Unlimited support</li><li>Client portal</li></ul>
TaxAct	<ul><li>Several options to import data</li><li>Data backup</li><li>E-filing, E-signature facilities</li><li>Audit Management</li><li>Mobile App</li></ul>
ProSeries	<ul><li>Has tool to find forms faster</li><li>Automatically transfers data to returns</li><li>Imports data from QuickBooks and other file formats</li></ul>

Chapter 12: Payment Software Options

One of the key features a small business needs to set up is a way to receive payment for services completed. While some people use checks or money transfers, most people expect businesses to have online payment options.

There are many options for online payment options, and most companies help you manage billing, provide payment processing, and store customer information for future billing. As well, the industry leaders have a mobile app that allows you to collect payments on the go, if you happen to meet people in person, or sell products or services at a conference, or in other settings.

As mentioned earlier, TaxDome is a system I use, and within TaxDome, you can set up payments through Stripe or CPACharge to process payments. One big benefit of TaxDome is that it offers you the ability to effectively lock the tax return from the client until the invoice is paid.

To avoid any issues around payments, consider including a payment authorization form in their onboarding package so they can agree to the terms and set up recurring payments from the beginning of the working relationship.

Other payment options include:

QuickBooks Online
CPACharge
Stripe
Square
PayPal Business
Cash App
Venmo Business

PART III

INVESTING IN YOURSELF: BUILDING YOUR SKILLS

TaxUSign

Chapter 13: Education and Learning

While these two terms are often interchanged, they are actually quite different, with different implications for you as a professional.

Education is the process you underwent to acquire specific, systemic instruction, like at school. There is curriculum and assessment, and you were educated on the topics of the subjects.

Learning, on the other hand, is the acquisition of knowledge or skills through study, experience, or being taught by others in your life, either in a formal capacity, like an employer or mentor, or informally, like gleaning new practices and ideas from peers or participating in professional development.

In this ever-changing field of taxation and finances, it is vital to invest in both your ongoing education and your commitment to lifelong learning to bring the best expertise to your clients.

Foundation	• Business Plan & Financial Projections • Strengths and Weaknesses • Likes vs Dislikes
Mindset	Whether you think you can or think you can't, you're right. ~Henry Ford
Investing in Yourself	• Training & Education
Building Your Skills	• Improve your skills
Step Out of Your Comfort Zone	• Challenging yourself
Lifetime Learner	• Never stop learning and growing

You might have gone to school to learn one area, but you aren't limited to staying in that one field forever. With education and learning, you can invest in your professional growth and expand your skills to offer new services to clients.

Bookkeeping	<ul><li>Accounting Software Set Up and Training</li><li>Set Up Chart of Accounts</li><li>Monthly Bookkeeping</li><li>Bookkeeping Review (Monthly, Quarterly, or Annually)</li><li>Catch-Up and Clean-Up</li><li>Financial Statement Review</li><li>Getting Financial Reports Ready for Tax Preparation</li></ul>
Tax Preparation	<ul><li>Individual tax returns</li><li>Business tax returns (federal, sales tax, and payroll tax)</li></ul>
Tax Planning	<ul><li>Financial Planning</li><li>Retirement Planning</li><li>Investment Planning</li></ul>
Tax Representation	<ul><li>IRS Audit and Collections</li><li>Innocent and Injured Spouse</li><li>Filing Back Taxes and Returns</li><li>Payroll Tax Issues</li><li>IRS Liens, Levies, and Seizures</li><li>IRS Wage Garnishment</li><li>Payment Plans</li></ul>
Advisory	<ul><li>Business Tax Advisory</li><li>Retirement Tax Advisory</li><li>Family Tax Advisory</li><li>Real Estate Tax Advisory</li><li>Estate Tax Advisory</li><li>Education & Compliance</li></ul>
CFO	<ul><li>Strategic Planning</li><li>Cash Flow Forecasting</li><li>Key Performance Indicators</li></ul>

Chapter 14: Memberships & Organizations

Benefits of Memberships & Organizations

One way many professionals discover and deepen their knowledge and networks is through memberships and organizations in the industry.

Some of the benefits of being a part of these groups include:
- Finding continuing education or skill development trainings
- Access to leaders in the industry
- Networking with others in the field
- Access to specialized information
- Updates about the latest tax changes or requirements
- Building community and collaborations to better serve clients
- Finding support for projects, launches, and offers

Bookkeeping	• American Institute of Professional Bookkeepers
Tax Preparation	• Western CPE • National Association of Tax Professionals (NATP) • American Institute of Certified Public Accountants (AICPA) • National Society of Tax Professionals (NSTP)
Tax Planning	• American Institute of Certified Tax Planners (AICTP) • Think Outside of the Tax Box
Tax Representation	• American Society of Tax Problem Solvers (ASTPS) • Tax Rep Network (TRN) • National Tax Practice Institute (NTPI)

PART IV

BUILDING YOUR SERVICES & MARKETING

Chapter 15: Building & Bundling Your Services

Some professionals decide to be generalists, providing guidance in many areas, while others choose to become experts in one or two areas. This is guided by several factors, including your interests, your skills, your strengths, and your hopes for the future of your business. Additionally, what you build and bundle in your offers will also be somewhat determined by what your ideal clients need and want from a tax professional.

Let's look at two people. Sam and Chris are both bookkeepers. They both work meticulously to record and maintain accurate records and complete specific financial tasks for their respective clients. Sam loves the work and the challenge of documenting complex business transactions. Chris feels the same as Sam, and likes the extra challenge of preparing tax returns so there is a possibility for Chris to invest in future training and development to become an expert in tax preparation.

Bookkeeping
Tax Preparation
Tax Planning
Tax Representation
Advisory
CFO

Chapter 16: Marketing & Advertising

Marketing is the process of getting people interested in your company's product or service. This happens through market research, analysis, and understanding your ideal customer's interests. Marketing pertains to all aspects of a business, including product development, distribution methods, sales, and advertising. Here are some key terms you need to know to market your business.

Elevator Pitch	Short statement (less than 60 seconds) to explain what you do.
Social Media	Websites or apps where people create and share content like short articles, photos, graphics, videos, or ideas for social networking.
Branding Photography	Branding photography is when you have a professional photographer take pictures of you, your team, or your office to represent your business to attract your Ideal clients. These photos are used on your website and any social media accounts.
Website	Complex or simple, most businesses need a website to inform visitors, detail services, boost brand recognition, and drive sales.
Logo	A business logo is a symbol of your company's identity. Your logo visually represents your business and what you offer.
Business Cards	The business card represents your company's brand and includes name, title, email, website, address, and phone number.
Google My Business (GMB)	(GMB) is a free business listing from Google where you provide details and photos of your business, like your location, services, and products. Information from your Google Business Profile may appear in Google Search, Google Maps, and Google Shopping.
Search Engine Optimization (SEO)	SEO is the process of getting traffic in search engines. It aims to improve your website's position in search results pages.

ADVERTISING & MARKETING
Elevator Pitch

An **elevator pitch** is short statement that is less than 60 seconds to explain what you do.

These questions can help you prepare:
- What does your company do?
- What makes your brand unique?
- What value do you add to your customers' lives?
- Why would someone want to work with your organization?
- How does your company solve your customer's biggest problem?

Write your statement and say it out loud, revising, revising, and revising some more. Ask others for input, and test your pitch out with prospective clients to see how it resonates with them. Don't be afraid to add in words that showcase your strengths, your work style, and your personality.

Here is an example:

Hi my name is Lily Tran, Enrolled Agent and Founder of TaxUSign. We are a virtual tax firm serving individual and small business clients across the United States. We provide tax assistance anywhere, anytime. Remember virtual tax help for whatever life throws at you.

Draft your elevator pitch here:

_____

_____

_____

ADVERTISING & MARKETING

Advertising and marketing can feel confusing or overwhelming to even the most seasoned small business owners. However, when we break it down into smaller bits, you can see that you can do a great job sharing your expertise and promoting your business.

One way to advertise and market your business is to share with people you know, and people you meet. In these exchanges, you can share your elevator pitch and explain how you help people with their business issues in a casual, conversational way. This is known as *one-to-one* marketing.

In order to make a bigger impact and spread your message and expertise farther and wider, you will need to consider *one-to-many* marketing. There are several ways you can do this:

1. Publishing articles and professional interpretations about newsworthy topics relevant to your field of expertise.
2. Write a book and promote it on your social media channels, as well as with your networking organization partners, clients, and professional contacts.
3. Teaching workshops and trainings about topics that are in line with your business services.
4. Speaking at meetings, conferences, and industry events.

In the one-to-many model, you have the opportunity to impact many people at one time, not just to promote your business, but also to showcase who you are as a business owner, and how your personal and professional values define your work style and your priorities. In most cases, people in the audience will approach you afterwards to start a conversation and ask for your opinion about an issue they are facing, which in turn translates into a potential new client.

ADVERTISING & MARKETING
Social Media

More than three-quarters of the world's population aged 13+ uses social media. Social media marketing provides a unique opportunity to connect with this massive audience on the platforms where they already spend their time.

Social media marketing happens on platforms like Facebook, Instagram, TikTok, and LinkedIn, and is when businesses post information about their products or services, educate others on topics relevant to the business, and connect with existing and potential customers.

Imagine you create an excellent tax resource for a workshop and share it with the twenty participants in the room. That's great, right? Now imagine you share that same resource on your social media channels, like Facebook, Instagram, and LinkedIn, and 20,000 people from around the country and the world view it, like it, and download it. That is the power of social media.

Social media is also a great way to share updates and interpretations on items in the news that might not make sense to everyone, such as changes to the tax code, shifting tax deadlines, or new requirements for deductions. You can post your thoughts about breaking news topics, and your prospective and current clients can ask questions and interact with you in your post, showcasing your expertise and helping others see your value.

While speaking for audiences and writing books are staples of thought leadership and can establish you as a leader in your area of expertise, social media marketing is faster and more far reaching as a tool for growing your audience and sharing your knowledge.

Networking Organizations

Being an entrepreneur can be lonely, and many small business owners choose to join a networking organization to meet others in the same boat, as well as grow their professional networks. There are a variety of organizations, from informal to very structured.

General business groups allow everyone who is interested in business networking to attend, with people from various overlapping professions. These groups usually meet monthly and often have time for mingling and relationship building. They may also hold meetings where guest speakers present information on important business topics or to discuss issues concerning legislation, community affairs or local business topics.

More structured organizations whose primary purpose is to help members exchange business referrals are known as *strong contact referral groups*. These groups typically meet over breakfast or lunch, and limit membership to one member per profession or specialty to minimize competition and maximize referral opportunities. Oftentimes, these groups have strict participation rules and require membership fees. However, the benefit is that you have every other member of the group referring your business to others in their network, helping your business grow.

Take some time to explore what kind of networking organizations are in your area, and decide what your goals are in participating, and how you can get the most benefit out of your membership.

Networking	<ul><li>Local Chamber of Commerce</li><li>Business Network International</li><li>Entrepreneurs' Organization</li><li>Rotary International</li><li>Meetup</li></ul>
Speaking	<ul><li>Toastmasters</li><li>National Speaker Association</li></ul>

Chapter 17: Referral Marketing

Referral marketing is a form of advertising where businesses encourage customers to recommend their services, products or experiences to other people who might also benefit. Not only does it deepen the relationship with your current clients, it allows you to build relationships with prospective clients who are already curious about your services or products.

If you are considering this method of advertising, there are some benefits that are worthy of noting:

1. There is little to no cost, depending on how you structure it. You might offer rewards, discounts, freebies, or other incentives, but many small business owners begin a referral program without added costs.
2. There is a high value in referred customers - as much as 16% higher than average customers which means that these referrals bring in more revenue over the course of their relationship with you. This is because they are starting the relationship with you from a place of trust and belief that your business can solve their problem.
3. There is more conversion in this type of marketing and advertising, versus other forms. When someone hears about a product or service from a trusted source, like a friend, celebrity, or influencer, they are more likely to make the same purchase. One study showed 63% of Gen Z rank recommendations from friends as their most trusted source.

As the world of marketing and advertising has evolved, referral marketing has evolved too. Nowadays, it is common for referral marketing to be an intentional advertising strategy using incentives and rewards for customers in exchange for successful referrals. One common reward is a small discount for future services or products, or an added bonus of extra value. This makes sense in a retail space because you can offer a 10% discount on a future purchase of a specific product, but how does it work in a service industry like finance, tax, or accounting?

REFERRAL MARKETING

There are two types of marketing programs to consider.

1. Business to business marketing programs.
2. Business to customer marketing programs.

1. Business to business marketing programs are longstanding programs where professionals refer potential clients to fellow professionals. For example, if you use a product or service that you recommend, you can offer it to your clients using a special discount code that is connected to your name, so you receive the recognition of sending prospective customers to the business you recommend. Recognition for you could come in the form of discounts or points in a loyalty program.

2. Business to customer marketing programs are perfect for referral marketing because of the trust factor that exists between the business and the customer. One example is a popular tax software company offering a 'refer a friend' program where the customer shares a special code with a friend, and that existing customer receives either a 20% off the filing of their federal taxes online, or a $25 gift card.

REFERRAL DATABASE

NEW CLIENTS

Tracking referral sources empowers businesses to make data-driven decisions, enhance their marketing efforts, and foster stronger client relationships, leading to increased brand awareness and growth.

DATE	NAME	SOURCE	NEW CLIENT
TOTAL REFERRALS			

PART V

SALES & ONBOARDING CLIENTS

TaxUSign

Chapter 18: Onboarding Overview and First Steps

Once you have signed a new client, it is imperative to welcome them into your business and provide them with everything they need to be successful.

Here are some initial steps to consider as you onboard your new clients. It is beneficial to automate as many steps as possible so everyone receives the same high level of care and service, and nothing is missed.

1. Send out welcome documents. This may contain an overview of your working agreement, the terms of the work, and a copy of the signed contract, and a Non-Disclosure Agreement if required. It should include payment terms, and non-payment consequences. It should also include expectations and milestones, as well as timelines for both parties. And finally, it should include termination procedures for either party for future reference.
2. Payment Authorization form. This form includes full name, address, phone number, bank and credit card information, preferred method of payment, signature, and date.
3. Send out the Client Intake Form (sample is on following page).
4. Share how you will communicate with each other, and expectations around communication.
5. Give access to any online resources, repositories, and shared accounts.

The backend of your business has onboarding activities you need to complete:

1. Gather data and add client to your Customer Relationship Management system to enable email communication and tag their account so they receive relevant email information or updates.
2. Add client to time-tracker system to document time spent on their accounts.
3. Add client to your project management system to stay on top of work required and status updates.
4. Assign any tasks to others in your business, or schedule tasks for yourself.
5. Create an online client portal where all shared documents are kept securely.
6. Identify other products or services that could benefit your client and set up a plan to share with your client at the appropriate time.

Chapter 19: Onboarding Clients: Forms and Scripts

Onboarding new clients is a fun and exciting process, yet can also provide stress if you don't have the systems and structures in place to welcome them and set them up for success.

In the following pages, you will find forms and scripts to get you started. As always, please customize the templates to serve your business and clients the best.

1. Client intake form template
2. Sample script for client intake: Individual
3. Sample script for client intake: Business

Notes

CLIENT INTAKE FORMS
Sample of New Client Intake Form

Intake Date:

Name:

Business:

Address:

Email Address:

a. How did you hear about [Company]?

b. Tell me about your business: how did you structure your business?

c. When did you start your business?

d. How many people own this business?

e. Do you have an Operating Agreement?
    Yes   No

f. What products or services do you provide (More Detail)?

g. Do you have a separate business bank account?
    Business Bank Account   Personal

h. How do you track income and expenses?
    Excel   Using Accounting Software (QBO, Xero, Sage, FreshBook)

i. Where do you operate your business? In your home?
    Yes   No

j. Do you have a city of _____ license?
    Yes   No (If the answer is no, they may need a city license)

k. Department of Revenue tax return monthly, quarterly, or annual?
    Monthly   Quarterly   Annual

l. What types of services are you looking for?

m. Do you have any Questions?

SAMPLE SCRIPTS FOR CLIENT INTAKE: INDIVIDUAL

" Hello, my name is _____ and I am calling from [Company].
How are you doing today?" (Listen to their answer and respond accordingly)

" I would like to ask you a few questions to get to know you and your tax needs."

General Questions:
- Single, Married, filing Separately?
- Do you claim any kids? How many?
- Do you own a home?
- Do you have any virtual currency?
- Do you have any foreign accounts?
- Do you own or sell any stocks?
- When did you last file your taxes?
- Find out more about their situation, what they need, etc.
- Do you have any additional questions that I can relay to [name]?

Make sure to get a copy of the client's last tax return.

"Thank you for your time.

I will get this information over to [name] and he/she will contact you via email."

Notes

SAMPLE SCRIPTS FOR CLIENT INTAKE: BUSINESS

" Hello, my name is _____ and I am calling from [Company]. How are you doing today?" (Listen to their answer and respond accordingly)

"To get started, I have a few questions to ask you to better understand you and your business needs."

Specific Questions:
- How did you hear about [Company]?
- When did you start your business?
- What is your business entity?
  - Sole Proprietor, LLC, S-Corp, or C-Corp?
- How many people own this business?
  - How many employees? Contractors?
- Do you have an operating agreement?
- What products or services do you provide?
- Do you have a separate business bank account?
  - How many?
- How do you track income and expenses?
- Do you operate from home? (yes/no)
- Do you have a city of _____ license? (If no, they may need a city license - take notes)
- Are your tax returns current?
- Do you report sales tax?
  - Do you file monthly, quarterly, or annually?
- What types of services are you looking for?

Make sure to get a copy of the client's last tax return.
"Do you have any questions?" (Take note of the questions)

"Thank you for your time. I will get this information over to [name] and he/she will contact you via email within 1-2 business days."

GROWING & SCALING YOUR BUSINESS: TEAM BUILDING

Chapter 20: Finding Staff

Most likely, you were the only person working in your business in the beginning of your business, but as you sign more clients, that might have to change.

While it is hard to hand over parts of your business to other people, especially parts that you have so diligently managed for so long, it is necessary for you to do so in order to scale and grow your business.

There is significant work and investment that must happen to grow your team, and as a business owner, you want to hire the best person for the job. While some small business owners try to hire friends and family in the early stages, to either save time or money, that often isn't the best choice.

Hiring is critical for the future of your business, and the right candidate can serve your clients and grow your business with you, bringing skills and talents that compliment yours.

The first consideration is to identify what you need in terms of skills, talents, abilities, contributions, and work style. Define the job, and even write a job description so you become clear on what you need at this time. From there, you can start to look in places where you will find people with the abilities you desire. Especially in service industries like taxes and accounting, many small business owners think they need another person just like them to grow their business, but upon reflection of the job description, they may realize they first need a data entry person, or an administrative assistant, or a salesperson. Once you know what kind of work needs to be done, and what skills someone needs to be able to do the work, you can begin looking for qualified candidates.

GROWING & SCALING YOUR BUSINESS
FINDING STAFF

To find the best candidates for your business, consider reaching out to colleges and universities for internship programs. If they have programs in accounting, finance, or other relevant fields, they will have a job board or know of candidates who may want to work with your business very much.

Conduct interviews and training sessions virtually using tools like Zoom, and provide the necessary software and resources for remote work.

Job Sites
Colleges & Universities Internship Programs
Social Media
Job Boards on Organizations
Asking colleagues and professional partners

Chapter 21: Employee vs Independent Contractor

There is a lot to consider when hiring help for your business. The first is what classification your new hire should take: employee or independent contractor.

An employee requires I-9, W-4, and state tax forms, as well as possible registration in company benefits like health care, pension or retirement programs, or other benefits. Independent contractors don't qualify for company programs, and simply require a W-9 form and a contract stating the details of the agreement. A small business owner might want to take the simpler path and hire independent contractors instead of employees, but there are strict rules around who is considered an employee and who is considered an independent contractor. Here is an overview, although there are many exceptions and these are not absolute:

Employees	Independent Contractors
Works for a single employer	Can work for multiple employers
Uses tools the employer provides	Uses own tools
Employer provides instructions	Has autonomy over how to do the work
Receives a W-2	Receives IRS Form 1099
Eligible for overtime hours	Can increase earnings with other jobs
Employer withholds tax	Files own taxes
Cannot deduct business expenses	Can deduct business expenses

Chapter 22: Team Building & Retaining Staff

Once you hire your team and integrate them into the workflow of your business, there are some items you need to consider to continue to build up your team and retain them in your company. Not only is it important to keep your staff with you for continuity purposes with your clients, but employee retention promotes the health and success of your company with all clients. If your employees leave your company, they take their knowledge and expertise with them, and leave a big hole to fill for the remaining employees, which adds significant stress and pressure.

Keeping employees in your company, and creating a positive work environment will absolutely boost your business. Happy employees have:

- high morale
- increased productivity
- higher quality customer experience
- increased employee engagement and positive culture
- reduced expense and investment of recruiting, hiring and training

When you prioritize team members and provide professional growth opportunities for them, you will see these benefits and so much more. So, how do you build your team and retain them as part of your business?

- Team meetings to keep everyone on the same page and to acknowledge wins
- Team building activities and fun events to strengthen professional relationships
- Holding fun and friendly competitions
- Creating incentives for work completion or hitting targets
- Regularly meeting with each employee to discuss performance and reward contributions with bonuses, title and/or salary promotions, other perks.
- Provide training for new procedures, practices, or systems so everyone can be successful in the upgraded expectation.

SLACK: Top rated software for communication with teams. Slack makes work more easily with everyone.

- Channels: Bring order & clarity to work, Create alignment
- Connect: Collaborate with teams at other companies
- Messaging: Communicate better with team
- Accessibility
- Notification feature
- Apps & Integrations: Connect with Google Drive, Office 365 & over 2,200 more
- File Sharing, Chat search
- Security: protect your data

VOXER: Voxer is a free app that combines the best of voice, text, photo and video messages for a powerful and personal messaging tool.

- Real time voice messaging
- Live & Recorded Audio
- Multimedia: Alongside voice, send text, photos, video, gifs, Share your location
- Safe & Secure
- Large Group Chats: up to 500 individuals or team contacts
- Message Recall - Pro option
- Voice-to-Text Transcription - Pro option

TRILLIAN: Trillian is modern and secure instant messaging for people, business, and healthcare

- Free Windows, Mac, and Linux desktop clients
- iOS and Android mobile clients
- Optionally chat right in the web browser
- Send messages, images, & files
- 1:1 audio calls
- Notifications feature
- Access chat history (not free)
- 1:1 video calls (not free)
- Screen sharing (not free)

Notes

Chapter 23: Payroll Programs and Providers

Payroll services are outsourced software solutions that help business owners pay their employees accurately and on time while complying with all tax laws. While there are many payroll programs and solutions, it is important to evaluate each offer against the requirements of your business as every software is different.

As a real world example of referral marketing, I want to share a business that has been an excellent partner for my business.

ADP is a leader in providing payroll support to businesses, and was listed on the 2023 Fortune® World's Most Admired Companies™ list again for the 17th year.

From its website: https://connect.adp.com/steven-thuyen

ADP is a comprehensive global provider of cloud-based human capital management (HCM) solutions that unite HR, payroll, talent, time, tax and benefits administration, and a leader in business outsourcing services, analytics and compliance expertise. Our unmatched experience, deep insights and cutting-edge technology have transformed human resources from a back-office administrative function to a strategic business advantage.

Other payroll providers include the following:
- Gusto
  - Use this referral link: https://gusto.com/?referral_token=lily817&utm_source=login
- GetPayroll
  - Use this link: https://getpayroll.com/why-getpayroll/referral-partnership/
- OnPay
- JustWorks
- CFS Tools

PART VI

RESOURCES

TOP 7 MISTAKES MADE BY ENTREPRENEURS AND SMALL BUSINESSES

1. Choosing the wrong business entity structure
Work with a qualified tax professional to decide what works for you and ensure the correct tax forms are completed.

2. Entering the wrong business classification code or 999999 on Schedule C
This can further increase your chances of an audit. Take the time to select the classification code that is most appropriate for your business.

3. Misclassifying Workers
This can lead to audit issues and payroll tax penalties. Issue a W-2 for every employee. If you paid anyone $600 or more during the year, you might need to issue IRS Form 1099-MISC to individuals and businesses. The IRS, WA Dept of L&I, and other agencies provide guidelines to help you know if your worker is an employee or an independent contractor.

4. Commingling business and personal funds
Keep your business and personal finances separate to avoid the IRS from questioning the integrity of the business entity or the transactions. The benefits of setting up a business entity to protect you from personal liability can be lost it so. Maintain separate checking and credit card accounts for your business to avoid tax and legal trouble.

5. Poor record-keeping
In preparing a proper tax return, you need accurate records of your books. Save receipts, deposit slips, invoices, bank statements, and other documentation to show your income and expenses. Use a good accounting software to record your income and expenses.

6. Missing tax deductions and credits
Maintain accurate records to avoid losing out on important tax deductions. In claiming the home office deduction, there are two ways to compute home office expenses: 1) actual expenses vs. 2) IRS simplified rate. Additionally, there are two ways to compute auto expenses: 1) actual expenses vs. 2) allowable mileage allowance for each vehicle.

7. Failure to pay and/or file on time
Forgetting about tax deadlines or not having the funds to pay your taxes may lead to penalties that will accrue until a return is filed and paid. Don't panic. Ask for an extension to file and pay as much as possible with your tax return to reduce the late payment fees and interest. Ask a qualified tax professional to help you with a payment plan for the IRS.

Quick Tips:
- Make sure employees are not being paid as contractors.
- Keep business and personal finances separate
- Report all income on your tax return
- Keep detailed, accurate books & records

Consider applying for a business credit card that offers rewards and perks. This is a great way to prevent co-mingling funds. Here is a list of business credit cards you can apply for:

Credit Card	Best For	Annual Fee	Rewards Rate
American Express Blue Business Cash Card	Best for Overall Business Credit Card	$0	1%-2% Cashback
Chase Ink Business Cash Credit Card	Best for Cashback: Bonus categories	$0	1%-5% Cashback
Chase Ink Business Unlimited Credit Card	Best for Cashback: Flat-rate rewards, no annual fee	$0	1.5% Cashback
Capital One Spark Cash Plus	Best for Cash back: Heavy spenders	$150	2%-5% Cashback
Capital One Spark Miles for Business	Best for Travel rewards: Flat-rate rewards	$0 intro for the first year, then $95	2x Points
The Blue Business Plus Credit Card from American Express	Best for Intro APR + AmEx Points	$0	1x-2x Points
Chase Ink Business Preferred Credit Card	Best for Overall travel rewards + big sign-up offer	$95	1x-3x Points
The Business Platinum Card from American Express	Best for Luxury travel rewards	$695	1x-5x Points
Bank of America Business Advantage Travel Rewards World Mastercard Credit Card	Best for Travel rewards: No annual fee	$0	1.5x-3x Points
Chase New Business Card! Ink Business Premier Credit Card	Best for Cashback: Large purchases	$195	2%-5% Cashback
Capital on Tap Card	Best for Fair Credit	$0	1.5%
Chase United Business Card	Best for Airline business Credit Card	$99	1x-2x Miles
Capital One Spark Cash Select - $500 Cash Bonus	Best for Sign-up bonus (cash back)	$0	1.5%-5% Cashback

RESOURCES
Record Retention Requirements

Business Records Accounting	Retention Period	Corporate Records	Retention Period
Accounts Payable	7 years	Board Minutes	Permanent
Accounts Receivable	7 years	Bylaws	Permanent
Audit Reports	Permanent	Business Licenses	Permanent
Chart of Accounts	Permanent	Contracts - Major	Permanent
Depreciation Schedules	Permanent	Contracts - Minor	Life + 4 years
Expense Records	7 years	Insurance Policies	Life + 3 years
Financial Statements-Annual	Permanent	Leases / Mortgages	Permanent
Fixes Assets Purchases	Permanent	Patents / Trademarks	Permanent
General Ledger	Permanent	Shareholder Records	Permanent
Inventory Records	7 years *1	Stock Registers	Permanent
Loan Payment Schedules	7 years	Stock Transactions	Permanent
Purchase Orders	7 years	Tax Returns	7 years
Sales Records	7 years	Tax Returns	Permanent
Tax Returns	Permanent	Forms W-2	7 years

Bank Records	Retention Period		
		Forms 1099	7 years
Bank Reconciliations	7 years	Cancelled Checks	7 years
Bank Statements	7 years	Bank Deposit Slips	7 years
Cancelled Checks	7 years *2	**Real Property Records**	**Retention Period**
Electronic Payment Records	7 years		
		Construction Records	Permanent

Tax returns can be audited for up to three years after
the filing, up to six years if the IRS suspects under-
reported income. Keep all records seven years after
filing a return. Electronic records are equal to paper.
*1 Permanent for last - in - first - out system
*2 Permanent for real estate purchases

Real Property Records	Retention Period
Leasehold Improvements	Permanent
Lease Payment Records	Life + 4 years
Real Estate Purchase	Permanent

RESOURCES
Record Retention Requirements

Employee Records	Retention Period
Benefits Plan	Permanent
Employee Files Ex-Employees	7 years *4
Employee Applications	3 years
Employee Taxes	7 years
Payroll Records	7 years
Pension / Profit Sharing Plans	Permanent

Individual Records	Retention Period
Bank Statements	7 years
Charitable Contribution Documentation	7 years
Credit Card Statements	7 years
Tax Receipts & Logs	7 years
Investment Purchase and Sales Slips	Ownership + 7 years
Dividend Reinvestment Records	Ownership + 7 years
Year-End Brokerage Statements	Ownership + 7 years
Mutual Fund Annual Statements	Ownership + 7 years
Investment Property Purchase Documents	Ownership + 7 years
Home Purchase Documents	Ownership + 7 years
Home Improvement Receipts and Canceled Checks	Ownership + 7 years
Home Repair Receipts and Canceled Checks	Warranty Period For Item
Retirement Plan Annual Reports	Permanent
IRA Annual Reports	Permanent
IRA Nondeductible Contributions Form 8606	Permanent
Insurance Policies	Life of Policy + 3 years *3
Divorce Documents	Permanent
Loans	Term of Loan + 7 years
Estate Planning Documents	Permanent

Here are some useful Resources:
- Government Sites
  - Federal Government
  - State of Washington
- Financial Sites
- Forms & Publications
  - Employees vs Contractors Test
  - Payroll for Employees
  - Contractors
- Additional Handouts
- Preferred Vendors

https://www.taxusign.com/resources

*3 Check with your agent. Liability for prior years can vary.
*4 Or statute of limitations for employee lawsuits

BOOKKEEPING CHECKLIST
Bookkeeping self-chekup

- ☐ Provide two-year comparison Profit and Loss.
- ☐ Provide two-year comparison Balance Sheet.
- ☐ Wages Paid to Employees, and provide 4th quarter payroll returns and
- ☐ W3s. Are payroll entries completed correctly with taxes broken out? Does total payroll for wages agree to the W-3?
- ☐ Did you issue any 1099s? If not, should 1099s be issued?
- ☐ Any assets valued at more than $2,500 each during the tax year? If yes, provide copies of purchase documents, loan agreements, trade ins etc.
- ☐ Did the entity dispose of or sell any asset during the tax year?
- ☐ Are purchased or disposed assets reflected in the balance sheet, including any trade ins?
- ☐ Does the prior year tax return match the prior year balance sheet?
- ☐ Are all balance sheet accounts reconciled through the end of the year?
- ☐ Are there any negative balance sheet balances?
- ☐ Are there any reconciliation discrepancies?
- ☐ Are there uncleared transactions more than 90 days old?
- ☐ Are there any "Ask My Accountant" items? All business expenses must be classified to appropriate accounts. Do not classify expenses in other business expenses and miscellaneous expenses.

Notes

YEAR-END SMALL BUSINESS CHECKLIST

Please provide the following documents below:

- ☐ Prior Year Filed Federal Tax Return
- ☐ Business Licenses
- ☐ December 31st - Balance Sheet
- ☐ Gross Income and Expenses
    - ☐ January 1st through December 31st - Profit & Loss
- ☐ Wages Paid to Employee
    - ☐ W-3 & W-2s
    - ☐ Federal and State Payroll Returns (Form 941, Form 940, etc)
- ☐ Did you make any payments in this year that require you to file Form 1099?
    - ☐ Yes ☐ No
    - ☐ If Yes, did you or will you file required Forms 1099?
- ☐ WA Department of Revenue Tax Returns (if you are a retail-based business)
- ☐ December 31st Bank & Credit Statements
- ☐ Inventory: (If you are a retail-based business)
    - ☐ Beginning Inventory
    - ☐ Inventory Purchases
    - ☐ Items Removed for Personal Purposes
    - ☐ Ending Inventory
- ☐ Home Office:
    - ☐ Total Square Feet of Office Space
    - ☐ Total Square Feet of Home
    - ☐ Total expenses from January 1st through December 31st for mortgage interest or rent paid, utilities, etc.
- ☐ Business Use of Vehicle: (If you use your vehicle(s) for business)
    - ☐ Mileage Log with beginning & ending odometer reading
    - ☐ Types of Vehicles
    - ☐ Date in Service for each vehicle
    - ☐ Total Miles
    - ☐ Total Business Miles
    - ☐ Total Commuting Miles, Mileage Log
    - ☐ Amount of Parking and Tolls Paid
- ☐ Depreciation:
    - ☐ Cost and acquisition date of assets
    - ☐ Sales price and disposition date of any assets sold
- ☐ All business expenses have been classified to appropriate accounts. Do not classify expenses in other business expenses and miscellaneous expenses. Unknown expenses can be classified as "***Ask my Accountant***."

Continuing Education and Network Building

There are a variety of continuing educational programs to grow your skills and your network. Below is just a small assortment:

Mentorship	• TaxUSign - Academy Program Find more information at www.taxusign.com
Become an Enrolled Agent	• TaxMama (More information on following page) • Passkey • Gleim
Become a Certified Public Accountant	• Becker • Gleim
Become a Certified Tax Coach/Planner/ Strategies	• American Institute of Certified Tax Planners
Specialize in Tax Representation	• American Society of Tax Problem Solvers (ASTPS) • Tax Rep Network (TRN) - https://taxrepllc.com/tran • National Tax Practice Institute (NTPI)

Do you dream about running a virtual office of your very own?
Does the idea of having a successful business give you chills?
Do you want freedom to work how and where you want?

While this book will get you started, you might want more support to feel ready.
I've got you!

The Business in Box: Academy Program is a coaching program tailored to meet the needs of bookkeepers and tax professionals who want to start, grow, and scale their own virtual firms. The program is designed to offer a step-by-step roadmap for achieving these goals.

What You're Getting over a four week period:
- Six Hours of Educational Self-Paced Videos with Lessons and Homework
- Four Hours of Group Coaching, with time for Q&A
- Companion Book
- One Specially Selected Book on Bookkeeping and Taxes
- Access to Key Templates, Worksheets, and Checklists
- Preferred Vendor List for Setup Success
- Lifetime Access to Videos and Online Community
- Collaboration Opportunities
- Eligible for Referrals
- Discounts on Software and Programs

Training Overview:
Week 1: Setting Up Your Virtual Office + Coaching Session
Week 2: Investing in Yourself: Building Your Skills + Coaching Session
Week 3: Pricing & Packaging and Marketing + Coaching Session
Week 4: 1:1 Onboarding Training Session + Coaching Session

Through the self-paced video courses and the weekly group coaching calls over the four-week period, you will have ample opportunity to explore all the offerings in this program and establish your business to start serving clients of your own!

Visit www.taxusign.com for more information and registration.

TaxMama.com
Tax Information With A Mother's Touch

Congratulations on getting such a good foundation in bookkeeping!

Understanding these concepts is critical if you're going to build a practice around business clients – which is where you get your steady income.

In addition, this foundation will help you understand the important concepts when it comes to passing part of the EA Exam (IRS Special Enrollment Examination).

Once you master Lily's course, your next step should be to join TaxMama® and get the additional credential and authorities granted to Enrolled Agents (EA). As an EA you can provide valuable help to your clients when they face IRS or state audits, balances due, or notices that just keep coming and coming. You can stop IRS and state levies for clients who couldn't reach the IRS in time, after getting notices. And so much more.

Make this the year that you really round out your skills and become more profitable than ever.

Go to https://irsexams.school/signup/ use discount code LILY18 to get 18% off.

TaxUSign

ASTPS
American Society of Tax Problem Solvers

The American Society of Tax Problem Solvers (ASTPS) offers live technical training conferences, case support & continuing education through membership, and certification opportunities for practitioners looking to specialize in tax problem resolution.

They host a community of over 1,600 professionals from across the United States that specialize in representing taxpayers before the IRS and other taxing authorities. Membership in ASTPS reflects commitment to excellence and high standards in taxpayer representation.

"As a premium member of ASTPS, I've found their support and expertise invaluable. Their personalized services have saved me time on research. I highly recommend ASTPS to fellow professionals seeking top-tier tax problem resolution." - Lily Tran, EA

It's with a heavy heart that I share the sad news from the tax community: my dear friend, Eva Rosenberg, known as TaxMama, passed away on August 31st, 2023.

For those who knew TaxMama, she tirelessly guided numerous students to become Enrolled Agents (EAs) and raised public awareness about their vital role.

To honor her legacy, I am dedicating August 31st as "TaxMama Day." On this day, consider volunteering, spreading the word about EAs, or assisting aspiring EAs.